KU-253-092

Lake GARDA

Editions KINA ITALIA

Lake Garda

LAKE GARDA

Lake Garda is an island of scenery without compare, a mediterranean spot immersed in the savage grandeur of the alpine mountains. It is a combining of remote historic events and of human history.
Nature and history come together said Carlo Cattaneo, describing in 1844 this corner of paradise: "amazement would take the traveller to an even higher level if, on coming down from the summit of Baldo, where he had been gathering Bavarian sandstone plants, the pallene spinosa, citiso purpureo, he could already notice among the cracks in the rocks of the banks of lemon the flamming masses of oleander; and in the merry amphitheatre of Bogliaco he would even see, as if among the immense colonnades of Persèpoli or Menfi, the bizzare constructions of the citrus plants. He would see among the long walls of the extremely vaguely defined Salodiano countryside the nestling growth of the delicate flower of the Capparis and a continous forest of bay trees, with the odd cedar and orange tree, whose bright foliage alternates with the austere tints of the grey olive-groves strewing balmy gold under a limpid sky". A place where the interference of man has been respectful of nature, the environmental beauty reaches levels it would be difficult to surpass; like the "green Sirmio" which "smiles in the clear lake, flower of the peninsulas".

GEOGRAPHY
Lake Garda is situated 65 metres above sea level; it has a length, from the bank at Peschiera, of 51.6 km; it has a maximum width of 17.2 km; a perimeter of 155 km, a surface area of 389.98 km^2: the maximum depth (between Muslone and Castelletto di Brenzone)

is 346 m; the average depth is 135 m. The principle tributary is the Sarca which exiting near Peschiera takes the name Mincio. An artificial drainage system, to the north of the lake, near Torbole, directs the water from the Adige into Garda during the periods of high water level. The waters of the lake are also added to by numerous torrents, as well as underground waterways. Among these it is worth pointing out the Bojola spring which spouts near Sirmione. This is virgin water with volcanic origins which gushes out of the living rock at the bottom of the lake, at a depth of 19 m, with a temperature of 69.9 °C this water has healing powers noted since 1500. Lake Garda is bordered to the east by Mount Baldo which separates it from the valley of the Adige; to the west by a chain of steep mountains which give it the look of a fijord, into which open impressive bays, to the south by a line of morainic hills which run from Salò up to the foot slopes of mount Baldo. Picturesque roads run along all banks of the lake (particularly characteristic of the western area of Garda) while others branch off inland, offering to the tourists the possibility to reach enchanting places. 200 metres from the headland of S. Felice, in Valtenesi, is situated the isola del Garda, the largest and most important among those which dot the surface. It is 110 metres long and has a medium width of 65 metres. The characteristic winds of Garda: the Sover or Suer (called Bali on the bank of Trento) which blows from the mouth of the bank and disappears towards S. Vigilio. The Ander is often violent, it blows from west to east and brings good weather when it begins after midday and stops before sunset, bad when it goes on during the morning; it predicts a change in the weather. The Avreser (Balestro) it blows

LAKE GARDA. Gardesana Occidentale. (West Side).

from every part and brings diffuse clouds and changes and mixed weather. The evening winds are called Montesè, which means mountainous. From the west comes the Ora which is a regular wind and helps navigation. The Rèfol is a spring wind, sudden and short (which el moresa, meaning flirts). From the gableboard, in the winter arrives the Gardesana of Grancher or Luganot: it brings fog or variable weather. From the mouth of Vobarno (above Salò) comes the Bovaren which brings cold weather. Administratively Garda belongs to three regions (Lombardy, Veneto and Trentino) and to three provinces (Brescia, Verona and Trento). The villages of the lake are grouped into one community (community of Garda).

THE ORIGINS

Antonio Stoppani, on the origins of Garda, put forward a fascinating hypothesis: a marine fjord reemerging in the pliocene period. The more modern scientists however seem to be agreed on the "sinclinale benacense" (the concave extension taking place in the miocene period) and on excavations by ice the quarternery period. In the neogenic period the "fato benacense" was established: the characteristc contrast between the Brescian and Veronese banks; the design of the picturesque cliffs, with the violent aspects of the precipices. Garda, however, up until the end of the pliocene period, in spite of the forming of some particulars, did not yet exist in its real appearence. It took four quaternary glaciations, which scoured out, with repeated excavation works, the basin well over its length to bring in the crumbly rocks of the "sinclinale benacense". The ice, with varying advances and withdrawls, gave form to the moreniac hills which to the south, towards the plain, enclose the gardesian basin, with a festoon of multiple hoops. This fascinating chapter on the geological history of Garda is still being enlarged by the scholars in order to understand its full importance. There has also been put forward the hypothesis of a fifth glaciation - Donau - reemerging over seven-hundred thousand years ago. In this temporal dimension it is not easy to understand the sense of deep changes, the climatic ups and downs, which first of all, between one glaciation and another determined the vegetative development and afterwards the multiplication of fauna and the very living possibilities of man.

THE FLORA

Through the millenniums of geological history to our days the benacense (area around lake Garda) landscape is determined by a series of factors: the position at only 65 metres above sea level; the moderating action of the water (389 km^2 of surface with a volume of almost 50 km^3) on the temperature of the air; the barriers of mountains that protect it from the north winds; the relatively modest amount of water brought in by the tributaries and thus the limitation of the refrigerating effect on the mass of water (recently however controversies have arisen as to the possibilities of grave ecobiological mutations due to the dumping through the artificial canal at Torbole); the low rainfall (between one thousand and one thousand two hundred millimetres a year) with concentrated precipitation mostly in the spring or in the autumn; stable thermic values (mild summer temperature and high winter one). For these reasons many characteristics of the climate of Garda resemble the sub-mediterranean ones of the Ligurian Riviera. The mild winter temperature permits the flowering of numerous periwinkles, heather, daises, and small geraniums. The spring comes early: in March the mild weather is already inducing to outdoor life. The summer is long, dry and bright. The autumn is short, with the characteristic autumn rains. It is therefore noticeable that the general mediterranean character, acquires particular value according to the naturai position (the inlets, sheltered from the winds, on the southern shores; the hot, rocky slopes to the north) which favour a noticeable variety of vegetation .

THE FAUNA

The terrestrial fauna of Garda was almost completely destroyed with the dissapearence of the last secular forests. Once many zones (The Valtenese, mount Baldo, the mountainous inland area of the western bank) were the home of deer, roe deer, wolves and wild boars; not to mention the flying species which from the water to the summits of the morainic hills to the south and the high areas along the two main banks, were the naturalists joy. A small, but interesting sample, of winged species from the gardesan zone can still be admired in the collection preserved by the ancient abbey of Maguzzano di Lonato. The ignorance of man now seems to be completing its destructive cycle, speeding up the mortality among the more rare species of fish, with the alterations in the equilibriums of the water. This is the case with the Garda carp (Salmo carpio): only prompt action based on exact ecological knowledge could now ensure its survival.

HISTORY

The mild climate, the beauty of the countryside, the richness of nature — luxuriant woods, populated by a rich and varied fauna — all aided in the setting up of the first human settlements. The earliest traces of the presence of man are carved on the rocks of mount Baldo (a recent discovery). Who these first inhabitants were is not known. On the other hand the lives of other ancient inhabitants can be traced out more clearly — we take this note from one of the synthesis written by the historian Antonio Fappani — they left clear traces in the prehistoric settlements of Polada and in the peat bogs of Polpenazze (where even a prehistoric piragua was found) as well as those found at Desenzano, Bor,

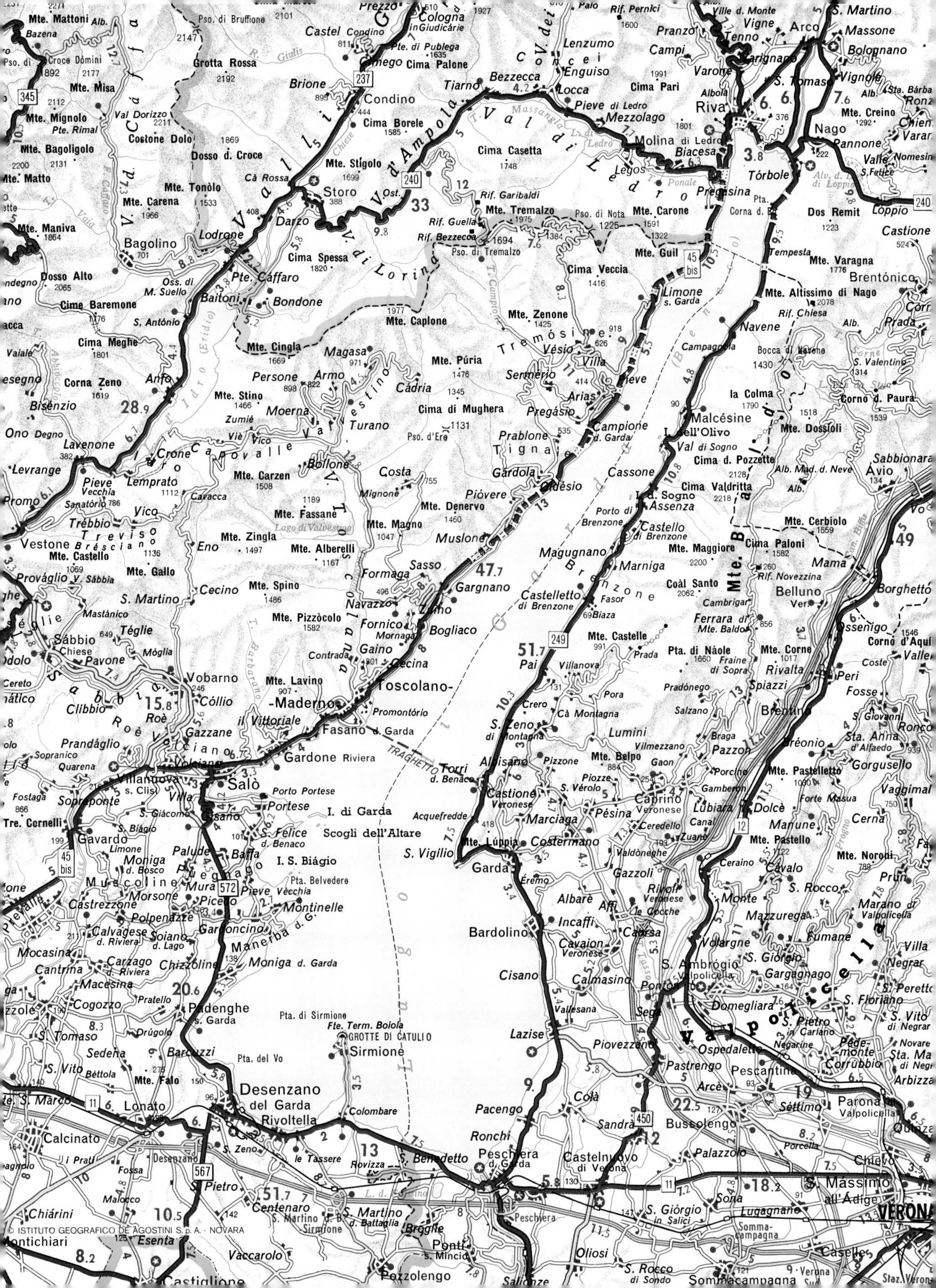

Mte. Mattoni
Bazena
Croce Dòmini
Mte. Misa
Mte. Mignolo
Pte. Rimal
Mte. Bagoligolo
Mte. Matto
Mte. Maniva
Pso. di Bruffione
Grotta Rossa
Costone Dolo
Dosso d. Croce
Cà Rossa
Mte. Tonòlo
Mte. Carena
Bagolino
Val Dorizzo
V. d. Cà ffa ro
Castel Condino
Cologna in Giudicàrie
Pte. di Publega
Cimego
Cima Palone
Brione
Condino
Cima Borele
Mte. Stigolo
Storo
Darzo
Lodrone
Cima Spessa
V. d. Ampola
Tiarno
Bezzecca
Val di Ledro
Lenzumo
Concei
Enguiso
Locca
Pieve di Ledro
Mezzolago
Molina di Ledro
Biacesa
Cima Casetta
Rif. Garibaldi
Mte. Tremalzo
Rif. Guella
Rif. Bezzecca
Pso. di Tremalzo
Pso. di Nota
Mte. Carone
Pregasina
Rif. Pernici
Pranzo
Campi
Varone
Cima Parì
Albola
Riva
Ville d. Monte
Vigne
Tenno
Arco
Varignano
S. Martino
Massone
Bolognano
S. Tomaso
Vignole
Sta. Bàrbara
Mte. Creino
Nago
Pannone
Valle
Tórbole
Alv. d. Loppio
Loppio
Dos Remit
Castione
Corna d. Bò
Mte. Guil
Tempesta
Mte. Varagna
Brentónico
Dosso Alto
Oss. di M. Suello
Pte. Caffaro
Baitoni
Bondone
V. di Lorina
Cima Veccia
Limone s. Garda
Mte. Altissimo di Nago
Rif. Chiesa
Navene
Cime Baremone
S. Antònio
Cima Meghe
Mte. Cingla
Mte. Caplone
Mte. Zenone
Tremósine
Vésio
Villa
Pieve
Sermerio
Arias
Campagnola
Bocca di Navene
S. Valentino
Corna Zeno
Anfo
Lago d'Idro
Magasa
Persone
Armo
Cadria
Mte. Púria
Mte. Stino
Moerna
Zumié
Turano
Cima di Mughera
Pregásio
Campione d. Garda
la Colma
Malcésine
Corno d. Paura
Mte. Dossioli
Bisénzio
Ono Degno
Lavenone
Crone
Capovalle
Vico
Pso. d'Ere
Prablone
Tignale
I. dell'Olivo
Val di Sogno
Cima d. Pozzette
Sabbionara
Avio
Levrange
Pieve Vecchia
Lemprato
Mte. Carzen
Bollone
Costa
Mignone
Gardola
Oldésio
Cassone
Alb. Mad. d. Neve
Cima Valdritta
Promo
Sanatório
Cavacca
Mte. Fassane
Lago di Valvestino
Mte. Denervo
Mte. Magno
Piòvere
I. d. Sogno
Assenza
Porto di Brenzone
Castello di Brenzone
Trébbio
Treviso Bresciano
Vestone
Mte. Castello
Mte. Zingla
Eno
Mte. Alberelli
Muslone
Magugnano
Mte. Maggiore
Cima Paloni
Mte. Cerbiolo
Mte. Gallo
Provàglio V. Sàbbia
Formaga
Sasso
Gargnano
Brenzone
Marniga
Rif. Novezzina
Mama
Belluno Ver.
Borghetto
Cecino
Mte. Spino
S. Martino
Mastánico
Navazzo
Zuino
Castelletto di Brenzone
Fasor
Coàl Santo
Cambrigar
Ferrara di Mte. Baldo
Mte. Pizzòcolo
Fornico
Mornaga
Bogliaco
Biaza
Ossenigo
Téglie
Sàbbio Chiese
Pavone
Móglia
Contrada
Gaino
Cecina
Mte. Castelle
Prada
Pta. di Nàole
Fraine di Sopra
Mte. Corne
Rivalta
Peri
Corno d'Aquilio
Vallene
Vobarno
Cóllio
Mte. Lavino
Toscolano-Maderno
Promontório
Pai
Villanova
Pradónego
Spiazzi
Coste
Fosse
Clìbbio
Roè Volciano
Gazzane
il Vittoriale
Fasano d. Garda
Crero
Cà Montagna
Pora
Salzano
Brentino
S. Giovanni
Roncone
Prandáglio
Sopranico
Quarena
Gardone Riviera
Traghetto
Torri d. Benaco
S. Zeno di Montagna
Lumini
Vilmezzano
Braga
Pazzon
Sta. Anna d'Alfaedo
Bréonio
Villanuova s. Clisi
Volciano
Salò
Porto Portese
Portese
Albisano
Pizzone
Mte. Belpo
Gaon
Porcino
Mte. Pastelletto
Gorgusello
Fostaga
Soprapponte
Villa
Gàrdola
S. Giácomo
Gisano
I. di Garda
Castione Veronese
Piozze
S. Vèrolo
Caprino Veronese
Gamberon
Lubiara
Dolcè
Forte Masua
Vaggimal
Tre. Cornelli
Gavardo
S. Biágio
S. Felice d. Benaco
Scogli dell'Altare
Acquefredde
Marciaga
Pésina
Ceredello
Canal
Zuane
Manune
Cerna
Limone
Moniga d. Bosco
Palude
Baffa
I. S. Biágio
S. Vigilio
Mte. Lúppia
Costermano
Valdoneghe
Mte. Pastello
Mte. Noroni
Muscoline
Puegnago
Mura
Pta. Belvedere
Pieve Vecchia
Garda
Éremo
Gazzoli
Rivoli Veronese
Cavalo
S. Rocco
Prun
Castrezzone
Morsone
Picedo
Montinelle
Albarè
Affi
le Cocche
Monte
Marano di Valpolicella
Polpenazze
Calvagese d. Riviera
Soiano d. Lago
Gardoncino
Incaffi
Bardolino
Caorsa
Mazzurega
Fumane
Mocasina
Manerba d. G.
Cavaion Veronese
Volargne
Villa
Negrar
Cantrina
Carzago d. Riviera
Chizzoline
Moniga d. Garda
Cisano
S. Ambrógio Valpolicella
S. Giorgio
Gargagnago
Macesina
Calmasino
Ponton
Sta. Perretta
Cogozzo
Pratello
Padenghe s. Garda
Pta. di Sirmione
Vallesana
Sega
Domegliara
S. Floriano
S. Vito di Negrar
S. Tomaso
Sedena
Drúgolo
Fte. Term. Boiola
Grotte di Catullo
Sirmione
Lazise
Piovezzano
Valpolicella
Ospedaletto
S. Pietro in Cariano
Negarine
Pedemonte
Corrùbbio
Novare
Sta. Maria di Negrar
S. Vito
Bettola
Mte. Falo
Barcuzzi
Pta. del Vo
Pastrengo
Pescantina
Arbizzano
Mte. S. Marco
Lonato
Desenzano del Garda
Rivoltella
Colombare
Colà
Arcè
Paronа Valpolicella
Calcinato
Pacengo
Sandrà
Bussolengo
Séttimo
Quinzano
Desenzano
S. Zeno
le Tassere
Rovizza
S. Benedetto
Ronchi
Peschiera d. Garda
Castelnuovo di Verona
Palazzolo
Porcilla
Chievo
i Prati
Fossa
S. Pietro
Centenaro
L. d. Frassino
S. Martino d. Battaglia
Peschiera
S. Giórgio in Salici
Sona
Lugagnano
S. Massimo all'Adige
Verona
Chiárini
Malocco
S. Martino d. B.
Sirmione
Broglie
Ponti s. Mincio
Somma-campagna
Montichiari
Esenta
Vaccarolo
Oliosi
Caselle
Castiglione
Pozzolengo
Salionze
S. Rocco di Sondo
Sommacampagna
Verona
Staz. Verona

© ISTITUTO GEOGRAFICO DE AGOSTINI S. p. A. - NOVARA

Pacengo, Bardolino, Cisano etc. The Ligurians and the Euganians accompanied or substituted, the Etruscans, the Enetites, the Isarcs, the Erectus and the Celts. Then it was the turn of the Cenomanes who took over from the aboriginal population. This continous alternation of the ancient inhabitants can be reconstructed using the toponyms and gravestones, like the relatively famous one by Voltino with the bilingual inscription. The very name Benaco, according to some scholars of celtic origins, derives from benncorno, peninsula peak and must therefore signify "lake of the peninsulas".

The Romans in 152 B.C. drove out or subjugated the Cenomanes; in 89 B.C. they conceded the latin law to the Transpadians and fourty years later Roman citizenship. The western bank of the Riviera, up to the northern limits (including the territory of Arco) was ascribed to the Fabia tribe; the eastern bank (together with Verona) was passed to the Polibia tribe. The Garda basin, from then on, was almost always divided into two or three administrative departments. The testimony to the Romans on Garda is impressive: from Sirmione to Desenzano, to Salò; from Toscolano to Riva, monuments, both large and small, on Garda document an era of intense and splendid life. Not even the barbaric invasions (Ostrogothic, Gothic, Alemannian) succeded in eliminating them; as did neither the successive Byzantine and Longobard dominations (the latter was relatively important).

In this era the first spreading out of christianity was noted with the work of some bishop-saints (S. Vigilio, S. Euprerio, and especially S. Ercolano). Thus the first christian communities sprang up at Tremosine, Castelletto di Brenzone and Sirmione, as the most ancient churches show.

The Carolingian domination, following the Longobardian one, had to give in to the barbaric invasion for the holding back of which in the IX century A.D. the fortified enclosures were built (some of which are still visible today) in Padenghe, Moniga, Maderno, Lonato etc. In 899 the Huns destroyed the monastery at Maguzzano which was rebuilt centuries later. The rock of Garda became the refuge of Adelaide, the widow of Lotario and later the wife of Ottone. The different emperors conceded numerous fiefs on Garda, while Maderno, Manerba, Salò and Desenzano took on particular importance in the infinite struggle between the various factions and the army forces. In the XIII century the Patarine heresy was particularly powerful on Garda (especially at Sirmione): its leader frà Dolcine ended up on the stake along with 170 followers on the 13th february 1278 at Verona.

The period of the communal autonomy was particularly vivacious, with singular decrees and statutes. It was also the open field of the struggle between the Guelfa and Ghibellina factions, between the signori of Ezzelino da Romano and the Scaligeri and the Visconti di Pandolfo Malatesta. In the XI century the traditional division on Garda between Brescia and Verona was established, the power of the bishop-prince of Trento who obtained on the 9th of February 1182, from the emperor Frederick I, the right of navigation. Ten years later, 26th-27th July 1192, the emperor Henry VI gave Brescia jurisdiction over all the territory on the central-western bank, from Pozzolengo to Limone. To free itself from the rule of the Scaligeri and the Visconti the community of Garda came into being in the first half on the XIV century, a confederation of the Brescian communities on Garda. After having resisted an attempted takeover by Cangrande and by Mastino della Scala, signori from Verona, the community consolidated its status placing itself under the protection of Venice and appointed itself in Magnifica Patria. The protectorate of Venice over the Riviera was relatively short: it lasted from 1339 to 1351. Then followed the disputed dominion of the Visconti di Milano which contrary to ending actually consolidated the autonomy of the Magnifica Patria, recognised in 1419 by the same Filippo Maria Visconti. Such autonomy — which was never indipendence — was reconfirmed by the Republic of Venice, when the Riviera made an act of dedication to it on 13th May 1426. In payment for the loyalty shown during the war against the army of Niccolò Piccinino, the Riviera became considered, by the serene Republic of Venice, as separate land together with Valcamonica, Asola, Lonato etc. The Magnifica Patria defended its autonomy even against the pretensions of Brescia. It only obtained however the symbolic right of nominating a mayor, a right which led to the difficult situation for which Venice installed beside the mayor a Venetian patrician with the title of "Captain of the Riviera and Supervisor of Salò". The Magnifica Patria continued, with these rules, up to 1797, tying its destinies irrevocably to those of Venice constituting a unique fact in the history of the Riviera which was not repeated either on the Veronese or the Trentine banks. On the Veronese bank, in the XI century, there came into being an administrative district taking in the coastal communities from Malcesine to Lugana, elected as a county in 1131, with real autonomy and a real territorial council. In 1193 the dominion of Verona spread along the lake: the commune of this city, acquired from Henry VI the rock of Garda, and extended its juridiction even to the community of Sirmione. The Veronese territory then passed under the rule of Ezzelino da Romano, under that of the Scaligeri and finally, in 1405, under that of Venice. The chain of events at the extreme north of Garda, was different: in the Longobard and Carolingian eras they had set up a Judicaria Summa Laganensis (the name has remained to the Valli Giudicarie) where the March of Verona and in 976 passed on to the power of the Benedictine mon-

asteries of Leno, Brescia, Bobbio, Nonantola etc. joined up, and assumed ever greater importance, with that of the bishop of Trento, it took the place of the March of Verona and in 976 passed on to the duke of Carinzia to then be returned, with the decree of Henry II on the 9th april 1004 to the bishop of Trento, raised to the position of prince.The donation was confirmed by Corrado II with a decree of the 31st may 1027. The bishop principality of Trento was thus made completely indipendent of any other jurisdiction. This dominion defended itself against the repeated attempts of control by the counts of Tirolo and by the Hapsburgs, until the 4th february 1803 with the annexation by the Austrians. In 1918 the population freed itself from this dominion to join Italy. The facts relative to the governing of the water are different to those for the land. Exclusive rights to it were bestowed on the Venetian republic, having Charles IV, in 1351, conceded to Mastino II della Scala, all the waters of the lake, with rights of navigation and fishing, rights passed on to the Viscontis, the Carraras, to the Scaligeris and thus to the Serene State of Venice in 1406. From 1426 to 1455 such rights on the waters were administrated by the supervisor and captain of Salò and after by the captain of Malcesine. The Trentine authorities, in the middle of the 17th century, contested these rights; however only in the 18th century was the dominion of the Hapsburgs set up on the southern part of the lake. The fall of the Venetian dominion was brought about by the Napoleonic armies in 1797.
Opposed to him and the army of the Brescian Republic were the Valsabbines who had come down towards the lake. Military action between the Austrians and the French took place between 1801 and 1805; however, despite the differences, the Riviera, in 1815 passed to Austria. Many patriots raised their voices against the Austrian dominion while between 1848 and 1868 the names of Pastrengo, Peschiera, S. Martino, Solferino, and Custoza became famous due to their courage and Italian blood. The history of the last hundred years is worthy of note: in 1848 Peschiera, which was part of the historic quadrilateral (with Verona, Mantova and Legnago), fell into Italian hands. On the 24th june 1859 in the hills of S. Martino and Solferino the bloody battle which liberated Lombardy from Austrian rule was fought. In 1866 the Austrian gunboats bombarded Gargnano and the Brescian bank at exactly the same time as Garibaldi's volunteers were climbing from val di Ledro towards Ponale and at Custoza they fought a tough and unfortunate battle which however won for Italy the whole Veronese bank. The high regions of Garda saw fighting between 1915 and 1918, until the Italian offensive liberated all the territories, the last act of unification.

NAVIGATION ON GARDA

The remains of prehistoric piraguas confirm that man has always navigated on the waters of lake Garda. Not until 1827, however, under the Austrian government was a regular navigational service inaugurated using the steamboat "Arciduca Ranieri" of 40 tons, with wharfs at Riva and at Desenzano. After the second war of indipendence the lake was divided into two: the northern half went to Austria the southern to Italy. The society of northern Italian railways substituted the old gunboat anchored at Sirmione (the service was every fifteen days from Salò to Sirmione) with four steamboats. Only in 1888, with the society Rete Adriatica, did two new steamboats enter into service. The service was strengthened and restructured in 1918 with the definite passing over of all the Gardanese coasts to Italy. The actual navigation service is under the management of the government with regular lines the whole year round and tourist cruises in the summer period.

LAKE GARDA. Panorama.

SIRMIONE

The castle or fortress was built as a stronghold by Mastino della Scala, within the confines of the ancient walls surrounding the whole Medieval hamlet. For line, structure and condition of conservation it is considered the finest of the surviving castles of the period of the Scaligeri. Downstairs you can see architectonic fragments and structures of different periods: from the Keep (146 steps) you enjoy a wonderful view of the town. From the inside staircases of the Keep you can reach the patrol communication trenches.
The peninsula of Sirmione leaning from south over the blue waters of Benaco for about 4 km is much frequented for the splendour of its landscape and for thermal treatments. The poets Catullo and Carducci, charmed by the beauty of these places, described them with immortal lines. The whole island (that joins the isthmus by a bridge changing it into a peninsula) seems a wide, wonderful natural park, run along by alleys and paths among a luxuriant vegetation of olive-trees, cypresses, laurels and magnolias. Three hills rise inside, the first, eastward, is called "Cortine" the second, westward "Malvino" the third northward, between the two, is called "Catullus's Caves" seat of the archaeological zone of an ancient roman palace.

HISTORY.
According to some scholars the peninsula probably derives its name from the ancient greek word "syrma" (tail, train) or from the Gallic words "sirm" and "ona" (aquatic hotel) The peninsula was

SIRMIONE.Scaligero Castle. (XIII cent.).

SIRMIONE. Characteristic views.

certainly inhabited from the remotest ages. The noticeable Roman buildings, the tombstones, the trunks of the columns, the capitals and other relics found during the centuries testify the ancient importance of Sirmione that is remembered as a town in Antonino's itinerary. The history of Sirmione doesn't stop at the Roman period. It was chosen by queen Ansa, wife of Longobard's King Desiderio, who build a monastery of the Benedictines in the VIII cent. Sirmione passed urder the rule of the Scaligeri who built the fortress "the second among the castles of Europa for purity of lines and conception ingeniousness". The castle, conceived as a fortification, surrounded all the hamlet by its walls. The Visconti succeeded the Scaligeri, later the Carraresi of Padua. At the beginning of the XV century, Sirmione passed under Venice, following its vicissitudes.

TO SEE.
The Scaligero Castle. Catullus's Caves. S. Maria Maggiore's parish church. S. Pietro Mavino's small church.

Archaeological Walk.
It starts from the panoramic road to the lake, with charming sights of the scenery on the background of the waters. In the open space from which we can reach the lake, there are important relics known as the Great Pillar and the Great Archways (four). On the right side (facing the archways) there is a short stairway leading to a large place with barrel vault (with four niches containing the last discoveries) called the Horse Grotto because here were unearthed some relics of a horse: in 1500 it was probably used as a stable. Climbing another stairway and turn-

SIRMIONE.Scaligero Castle. (XIII cent.).

SIRMIONE. Great St Mary's Church (XV cent.).

SIRMIONE. Great St Mary's Church (XV-XVI cent. fresco).

ing left we get to the Long Corridor on whose background there is the Three-mullioned Window of Paradise. Along this "corridor" we see on the left the Giants Room (so called because of the big stones found here), the largest area in the villa.

The Double Cryptoporticus.
Is the sector of greatest architectural interest. According to Dr. Mirabella Roberti — on whose guidance we have relied for these notes — the long "arcade, now without a roof, extended from one end of the construction, from N to S for 159 m and was composed of two corridors each 4.20 m wide, separated by a line of 64 pillars forming an arcade which supported two large barrel vaults (fragments can be seen here and there) in concrete with pieces of porous tufa". It was also used for taking a stroll on oppressive days. Situated on the outside are so-called Botteghe (shops) claimed, by those who disagree with Dr. Mirabella Roberti, to be the commercial area of the spa or possibly ruins of the longobard monastery of queen Ansa.

The Swimming-pool.
In a large rectangular place (18,30 m by 8,10) there are four flights of steps leading down to a vast pool. The large rectangular room was built later; it was heated by means of warm air which passed beneath the brick floor. It was the "tepidarium" of the villa's private thermae, close to it there were rooms for sweating ("sudationes") and for the cold bath (" frigidarium") .

The "Antiquarium".
The most precious relics are here collected, among which we have oil lamps, pieces of vases, fibulas, fragments of plasters, of decorative stuccoes, of frescoes (with

SIRMIONE.Scaligero Castle (XIII cent.).

SIRMIONE. Aeriel view, the "caves of Catullus" in the foreground.

fruit and birds, sacrifice scenes, female figures, etc.). Interesting is also the photographical report of the monumental complex and of the excavations.

S. Peter's Church in Mavino.
A very ancient church in Romanesque style. The first building goes back to the VIII century, in the following centuries (XI-XIV cent.) it underwent several modifications. It rises on the top of Mavino hill on the ruins of an ancient pagan temple. Inside, on the walls and in the apses there are valuable frescoes of the XV and XVI cent.

St. Anne's Church close to the Fortress.
This is probably the church that strikes the tourists more. It is situated just at the entrance to the inhabited area after passing the drawbridge, on the left side, leaning on the castle walls. The church — dedicated to St. Anne, the Virgin's mother — was built in the fifteenth century just to offer a religious service to the garrison of the castle and to the inhabitants of the surrounding area. It now belongs to the city hall and it is almost always open to the public, also by night. With its candles lighting up the votive image, it confers an evocative athmosphere to this wonderful area in Sirmione. Someone affirms it was first erected in the late fourteenth century, while the cross vault was built in the fifteenth century and the barrel vault is supposed to date back to the seventeenth century. The church has a single aisle and only one altar; the small presbytery, built in the eighteenth century, is decorated with stuccoes which break the harmony of the whole. The votive frescoes — painted by various artists date back to the early sixteenth century. The Virgin on the altar is painted on stone with the Scaligeri's armorial bearings.

SIRMIONE. St Anne's Church (XIV-XV cent.). Interior.

SIRMIONE. Caves of Catullus: arcades of the double cryptoportico.

SIRMIONE. Caves of Catullus: Roman remains.

DESENZANO DEL GARDA

The picturesque small town, placed on the south part of the lake on the famous homonymous gulf, has got the widest and best equipped port of Garda and the ancient, characteristic small port surrounded by buildings on three sides. Desenzano is the seat of the Navigation Company on the whole lake. One among the most important centres, it has had these years a large commercial, tourist and residential deveiopment.

HISTORY.
Desenzano was one of the first places inhabited by man in prehistoric times after the withdrawal of glaciers; the ruins of the Polada civilisation, discovered in 1873, on the way to Lonato, witness it. The prehistoric station discovered during excavations of peat is still wrapt in mystery, in spite of the numerous objects, tools and fossil remains come to light and kept at the Ethnographic Museum in Rome. The Roman period was particularly flourishing; it was the theatre of a victory on the Goths (269). We have many witnesses on that period such as the remains of a villa. It was invaded by the Barbarians and given by Charlemagne to the monks of S. Zeno in 879. It was a feud of Count Ugone and in 1426 passed under the Republic of Venice. After the fall of Venice it passed under Brescia of which it followed the destiny . The Venetian period was of great importance; in that period the

DESENZANO DEL GARDA. The small characteristic port.

DESENZANO DEL GARDA. The lakeside.

DESENZANO DEL GARDA. The port.

MAYER

weekly market became famous (still now it keeps on tuesdays), it was an occasion of exchange for all the regions with Venice. We must remember the school of full speed founded at Desenzano from 1927 to 1937 where Agello and De Bernardi, piloting seaplanes, conquered many speed records; a monument was dedicated to these pioneers in 1967. Among the famous personnages of Desenzano we remember Angela Merici (1470-1540), sanctified in 1807. She devoted to the girls' education founding the congregation of the Angeline. Giosué Carducci stayed at Desenzano, serving periodically on the Royal Lyceum Committee. Signs of this period can be seen in his poetical works.

TO SEE.
The Roman villa of the III cent. BC. S. Maria Maddalena parish church.

CHARACTERISTIC POINTS.
The old port, surrounded on three sides by buildings among which is the Palazzo comunale and that of the supervisor which is Venetian, works of Todeschini; the promenade.

The Roman Villa. This grand construction was discovered, or at least the most important part, relatively recently. That is at the end of 1921, in the area of Borgo Regio, now Roman excavations have been started. The name is quite important: Borgo Regio, it is presumed, could have been the original site of the city if this hypothesis is true, Desenzano would have arisen around an agricultural nucleus, concentrated around a villa. The most important part, which remained up to now, of the internal complex is the recreational quarter of the villa, with an almost square courtyard in the middle surrounded, at one time, by a portico with six columns on each side except to the north. To the west is the house's recreation rooms, the oecus, where particularly interesting mosaics have been found, such as the one commonly called "running animals". The door mosaics are the most singular and interesting aspect of this monument: the colours are extremely vivid; there are many illustrated scenes, set in relief in rich framings. Other mosaics have rich geometric elaborations; they are all unforgettable for their joyous palette. Long neglected, they are severely damaged, however the actual setting and protection allow an interesting view.

S. Maria Maddalena's Church goes back to 1480. It was rebuilt in 1586 according to G. Todeschini's project. The temple facade is in Doric with a Baroque door of the XVIII century. Inside, there are the very interesting Doric columns and the wood statue of the Magdalen of the XV century, the high altar of the XVIII century to the Redeemer with little statues inlays and rich decorations in polychrome marbles, valuable paintings by Zenon Veronese. D. Cignaroli of the XVIII century, by D. Riccio of the XVI century, by A. Celesti, a Venetian painter of the XVII century, temper works by G. Anselmi. In the Blessed Sacrement chapel there are four Corinthian columns and the valuable altarpiece "the Last Supper" by G.B. Tiepolo .

DESENZANO DEL GARDA. The port.

MANERBA

MANERBA. The magnificent wide gulf.

S. FELICE DEL BENACO. Sanctuary of our Lady of Carmine (XV-XVI cent.).
S. FELICE DEL BENACO. Frescoes.

HISTORY.
The ancient Minervae arx is today an important touristic centre which has developed mainly in recent years. There were settlements there even before the Roman era. However, the history of Manerba is closely tied to its fortress (of which, unfortunately, today nothing remains): it was the site, in 776, of the final resistance of the Longobards commanded by Cacone (nephew of King Desiderio, against Charlemagne). The fortress passed to Beniamino da Manerba and then to the Scaligera family, the Viscontis, and the Venetians until in 1787, having become the haunt of a band of criminals, it was razed to the ground by order of the Superintendent of Salò. Innumerable stories and legends have grown up around the fortress, the best known of which are those collected in the book "I Valvassori Bresciani" by the Brescian writer Lorenzo Ercolani.
Great importance is attached to the Pieve or Parish Church which goes back to the XI century, from which descended all the chapels of the Valtenesi area, later raised to parish churches with the exception of that of Padenghe. The Pieve of Santa Maria, with the vicus romano, is the earliest evidence of Valtenesi unity.

TO SEE.
The precipice above which the fortress towered (known as the "Rocca di Manerba" and similar, according to some, depending on the point from which it is viewed, to Dante's profile); in the village of Solarolo the XVII century parish church and the ancient Church of St. John which belongs to the Cavalieri Gerosolimitani; in Pieve Vecchia, the Church of Santa Maria della Valle, one of the oldest on the riviera of Lake Garda and the most precious monument in the entire zone.

S. FELICE DEL BENACO

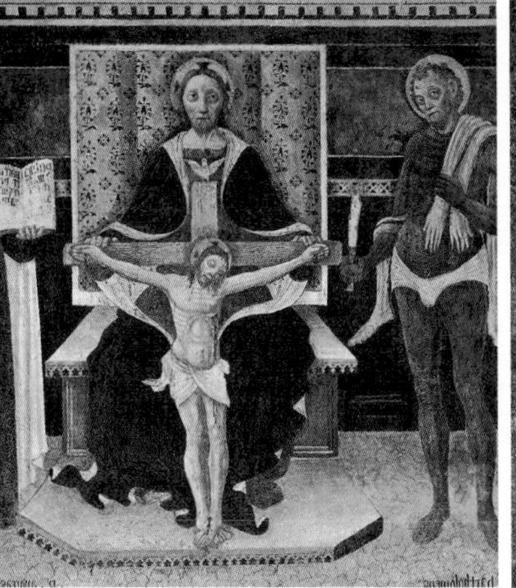

The Sanctuary of Our Lady of Carmine of the XV century. The building of medieval line, has a Romanic-Gothic architecture, with an ogive door and a bare central rosace. The building goes back to the XV century. The basilica shaped inside has only one nave with bare beams, divided by four ogive arches. The frescoes are interesting for the variety of subjects and styles of the XV, XVI, XVII cent. There are clear influences of Mantegna, Foppa, Perugino. There are noticeable paintings: a Madonna on the throne with the Baby of the XV century, a medieval style crucifixion in green land, four Saints ascribed to the Perugino's school and the Annunciation, a valuable work of the XV century.

HISTORY. An important centre in Roman times, S. Felice still has the characteristics of an agricultural district. Numerous signs of the Roman era remain, particularly tombs, one of which, dedicated to Neptune is walled into the east side of the bell tower of the parish church. The castle (of which only a few ruins remain) may have been built on the ruins of a Roman fort. Manara's volunteers who attempted to conquer the fortress of Peschiera, took refuge in it in 1848.

TO SEE. The XVI century parish church dedicated to Saints Felice and Adauto, built on the remains of a pagan temple, has some paintings of interest including one attributed to the school of Tiepolo; the Del Carmine Sanctuary, an interesting XV century construction which, from 1452, belonged to the Carmelo di Mantova monks, was suppressed by Napoleon, restored and reopened to the cult in 1952 by the same order. There are some interesting XV and XVI century frescoes to be admired there. Portese, a large and much visited village at one end of the Gulf of Salò, in an enchanting position and with the usual characteristic port; the "Baia del Vento" (Windy Bay), a picturesque inlet ending with the cape San Fermo (on which stands a fifteenth century church, the only remaining evidence of the older castle), extreme point of the S. Felice promontory at 220 metres from the Island of Garda.

SALO'

It is one of the most important commercial and tourist centres of the west Riviera of Garda. It lies in a wide, pleasant gulf on the slopes of mount S. Bartolomeo. From the neighbouring hills, rich in villas and olive yards, you can admire the grandiosity and beauty of the lake.

HISTORY.
According to a legend, Salò was founded by Queen Salonina or by Saloo. There are few evidences of the Roman Slodium, only some tombstones. In 1377 Beatrice Scala, Bernabò Visconti's wife, chose it as the capital of the "Wonderful Country" (Magnifica Patria). The statues "Riperiae lacus Gardae" stated the Podesta Salò had the title of Captain and had jurisdiction over the confederate centres. Beatrice della Scala propped up the walls and built a new castle, of which nothing remains at present. Sansovino built the palace of the Captain Rector (now the town-hall), while during the XV-XVI cent. the Duomo, a wonderful example of Gothic-Renaissance style, took its form. There are the two interesting entrance doors of the town (1463), one of the fortress toward Brescia and at the opposite end S. Giovanni's, within which the older part of the hamlet was enclosed. From the Autumn of 1943 to the Spring of 1945 Salò characterized the last period of fascism, known as the "Republic of Salò". Among the famous men who were born at Salò we must remember Gaspare Bertolotti (1540-1609) known as Gasparo da Salò, a famous maker of stringed instruments, inventor of the violin, whose bust, work of the sculptor

SALÒ. The lakeside at night.

Angelo Zanelli who planned also the Altar of the Country, is kept in the town hall.

TO SEE.
The Duomo in Gothic-Renaissance style of the XV-XVI cent., the Captain Rector's Palace, a work of Sansovino; the Clock Tower of the XV cent. In the cluster of houses of Barbarano there is Terzi-Martinengo Palace of the XVI cent. with a park full of fountains, built by the marquis Sforza-Pallavicino, admiral of the Venetian Republic.

The Cathedral. An original inscription dated the laying of the first stone back to the 7th October 1452. The designers — writes brother Ursula in the "Chronacle" — were ispired by the Veronese church of S. Aneastasia. The modifications undergone with time have not changed the unity of the building. There is an excellent equilibrium among the three aisles; with the cylindrical stone columns in relief; the crossed vaults either of the centrale aisle or of the lateral ones, are enriched with late-Gothic elements. The works of art are numerous: the grand polyptych — finished in 1476 — is by Bartolomeo da Isola Dovarese (the grand flowery Gothic frame) and by the Milanese Pietro Bussolo (among the statues which he signed is that of the Madonna with child). Also prominent are the statues and the crucifix on the ambones by Giovanni da Ulma (1400); the crib and the adoration of the Wise Men, by Zenon Veronese and Celesti respectively; the chapel of the holy sacrement is by the Cremonese Malosso (the right hand part is by Bertanza). In the baptistry there are works by Romanino. On the facade is the portal, never completed, which was carried out from 1506 to 1509 and attributed to Antonio della Porta and to Gasparo da Cairano.

SALÒ. Panorama.

SALÒ. Promenade and the landing-stage.

FRECCIA DELLE RIVIERE

GARDONE RIVIERA

It is one of the most elegant and beautiful zones of the lake for the variety and magnificence of its vegetation due to the mildness of the climate. It is a famous, international sojourn station lying among bright hills, large gardens, villas and sumptuous hotels. The inland favours interesting walks .

HISTORY.
The birthdate of Gardone Riviera is rather recent even if we have some proofs of an ancient past. The small town rose at the end of last century. Luigi Wimmer, a pioneer of the hotel industry, born in Germany, but fighting for the Italian Independence, gave it a peculiar impulse. He arrived at Gardone in 1880, took a liking to the place, characterized by a mild climate also in winter. He built hotels, urged different initiatives, created contacts with the cosmopolitan world. Year by year they formed the tourist Gardone with the promenade, the hotels, villa Alba, the Casino, buildings with different styles which testify the tastes of the cosmopolitan tourists who enlivened the small town at the beginning of the century. In 1921 the poet Gabriele D'Annunzio came to Gardone Riviera and settled at Cargnacco Villa, changed into the monumental complex of Vittoriale.

TO SEE.
The Vittoriale of the Italians; Hruska Botanical Garden.

GARDONE RIVIERA. The wet dock and the lake.

GRAND HOTEL

"IL VITTORIALE". The façade of the Priory, the Piave Pilium and the open air Theatre.

The Vittoriale of the Italians.
You can reach it from Vittoriale Square, very beautiful for the arch architectonic settlement. In front of the portal the scenographic architecture of the parish Church stands out.
After passing through the portal you reach the "Pilo del Piave" hung over by a statue of Arrigo Minerbi.
On the right there is the theatre in the open air (where every summer they perform ancient and modern plays). The landscape with the isle of Garda and the "Fortress of Manerba" is very suggestive. Advancing through an arcade you reach Esedra, where there is the small temple where Gabriele D'Annunzio was buried in 1963.
A narrow staircase leads to the Auditorium where the airplane Sva, by which the poet flew over Vienna on 9 August 1918, is kept.
On the right of the Auditorium there is the museum prepared in the building called "Schifamondo" where the life and work of Gabriele D'Annunzio is documented by antiques.
From the small balcony of the Auditorium you can see the Dalmatian small square, the heart of the Vittoriale with the Dalmatian pillar put on two large millstones to press olives. The building of "Schifamondo" shows itself on the square; eastward there is the Priory, the abode of Gabriele D'Annunzio (inaccessible to people) where the most authentic evidences of the Poet's life are kept.
Descending the stairs towards the lake you reach, on the right, the grave of princess Maria D'Annunzio di Montenevoso, the Poet's wife. In the portico of the Schifamondo there is the Fiat car, type 4, by which D'Annunzio guided the march from Ronchi to Fiume.
From the portico you reach the alley of Aligi leading to the "Fontanone del Delfino" where the water of a stream assembles.
On the right, behind an arch covered with ornaments there is the Mausoleum which keeps ten sepulchres, arranged in a ring, with the mortal remains of the Poet's companions in arms; in the central sepulchre, in 1963, they placed D'Annunzio's remains. On the south of the Mausoleum you can see the ship "Puglia" placed on an abutment, among the green.
The gardens are very interesting; you can reach them through a portal in the portico of the Priory.

"IL VITTORIALE". Aviation window (Museum); Study: where the writer worked; Sala del mappamondo (the Map Room) and detail of the prow of the ship "Puglia".

SQVADRA DELLA COMINA

TOSCOLANO-MADERNO

It is a very important centre formed by two towns, Toscolano and Maderno, blended into a single aggregate stretching on the Gardesana. Toscolano is prevailingly an industrial and a cottage-industry centre, while Maderno stretching in a picturesque gulf, with a wonderful promenade among villas and gardens is exclusively a tourist centre. It is much frequented for the mildness of its climate and its charming position.

HISTORY.
According to a legend, the ancient, mysterious town of Benaco, sunk into the lake owing to an earthquake (about 243 A.C.), was built near Toscolano. We know that near Toscolano there was a Roman oppidum: remains of a beautiful villa belonging to the Nonii-Arii Family came to light after several excavations.
You can find lapidary material of the villa in Verona on the facade of the Church. A memorial tablet on the bell tower, bears a dedication of the Benacensi to Marco Aurelio. In 1475 Gabriele di Pietro from Treviso, composed a "Donatus pro perulis" in Scalabrino Agnelli's printing house. Maderno was already in 969 a communal centre. Barbarossa granted it a conditioned independence. It was the chief town of the Riviera of Brescia till 1377 when Beatrice della Scala preferred Salò, which became the capital of the "Wonderful Country". About 1606 the Gonzaga of Maderno built a villa looking on the Gulf of Maderno. When it was left by the Gonzaga it soon went to ruin and nothing remains us.

TOSCOLANO-MADERNO View from Monte Maderno and characteristic view.

TO SEE.
The parish Church of Toscolano: it keeps 22 large pictures of Andrea Celesti representing stories of the Gospel and of S. Pietro. You can admire other paintings by Celesti, of biblical subject, in Delai Palace; the Roman Church of S. Andrea, at Maderno, of the XII cent.

The St. Andrew's Church (XII century). It is the Lombardian reduction of S. Zeno Maggiore, the greatest Romanic-Veronese monument. The facade mirrored three aisles inside; the moulding of the door with an arc in the dead centre closed by a lunette is — writes Gaetano Panazza — "rich and lively, among the most noble of the Romanic churches". The high and narrow window, still on the facade, recalls the Romanic windows of southern Italy. The inside with three aisles is where the greatest immediate variations are. Around the XV century three columns on each side were removed, they closed the monofore window and doors to build altars. The pulpit, placed against the second pillar on the left, is from 1565. In 1580, on the orders of S. Carlo Borromeo, the crypt was destroyed reducing the level of the church to its real state. Particularily curious is that on a block upturned in the corner a carved Roman biga can be seen, an obvious sign that in the construction of this church materials from buildings of an earlier era were used. The beautiful bell tower dates from 1469.

MADERNO. St. Andrew's Church (XII cent.). The harmonious façade is a masterpiece of lombard Romanesque architecture.

MADERNO. St. Andrew's Church (XII cent.). Detail of the Corinthian style capitals. An old fresco in the semicircle (Madonna and Child between two Saints).

MADERNO. St. Andrew's Church (XII cent.). The interior with three aisles.

MADERNO. Panorama.

GARGNANO

A characteristic, picturesque village placed among the green of the olive trees and the blue of the sky and the lake. Its environs are the goal of wonderful walks; a road leads to the lake of Idro, passing through the beautiful hilly zone of Valvestino.

HISTORY.
We have news of Cargnano already in 973; in fact, it is cited in a rescript for a donation to the cathedral of Verona. In the middle of the XIII cent. the Franciscans founded a convent and in 1285 built the Church consecrated to S. Francesco. In 1331 Giovanni di Boemia gave it as a feud to the Castelbarco. A century later the village became a part the "Wonderful Country" and the chief town of a "quadra" i.e. a group of villages. It was a prosperous centre for olive and lemon-growing and was improved, in the XVIII cent. by Bettoni Villa, one of the finest of Garda. During the "Republic of Salò" it gave hospitality to Mussolini and his family in the two Feltrinelli Villas. One of the two Villas, given to the University of Milan, is the seat of the Summer courses for foreigners.

TO SEE.
St. Francis of Assisi.
In 1289 the franciscans built a church of which only the heavily altered outside remains. The facade which is very similar to that of the church of St. Francis in Brescia, is divided by pillars into three par-

GARGNANO. The port and lakeside.

BOGLIACO. Bettoni Villa. Italian gardens by the architect V. Pierallini (XVIII cent.).

titions; the elegant stone portal has an arch with a full curve. The inside was redone in the XVII and XVIII centuries. The quadrangular cloister from the XIII century shows Venetian influence, with the rigid archs cast among the circular columns, which are decorated at the base with little protective foils decorated with cedar or lemon leafs of outstanding beauty.

The parish of S. Martino.
In the highest part of the village, climbing the little hills, the parish church is situated. According to the expert Conforti it rises on the site of a more ancient church. The primitive project of the parish would have belonged to a Trentine architect. In 1837 it was decided to trust its completion to Vantini, the celebrated architect who "inspired by the majestic, pagan temples, concieved a panthenon with an oval shape". The church holds paintings by Bertanza and by G.B. Casari, on the main altar there is a Madonna attributed to Moretto. Of the early architecture there remains the bell tower, which is of the Renaissance.

The eighteenth century Bettoni villa in Bogliaco, belonging to three orders, with abundant baroque grounds, the grand rococo stairways, the nymphs and statues by Domenico Cignaroli. The interesting paintings by Celesti are guarded in the hall.

Villa Feltrinelli (where Mussolini stayed for a certain period of time); the Church of the Crucifix in Bogliaco.

BOGLIACO. Bettoni Villa, main staircase. Architect A. Marchetti (XVIII cent.).

GARGNANO. The cloister of the convent of the franciscan Friars (XIII cent.).

BOGLIACO. Bettoni Villa. Central Hall. Frescoes by G. Galliari (XVIII cent.).

TIGNALE (m. 680)

A bright village with a tourist-agricultural economy lies down on a rocky tableland 600 metres high, and offers beautiful panoramas on the lake and the mountains. On a rock, perpendicularly to the waters, there is the sanctuary of Madonna di Monte Castello, overlooking all the south basin of the lake. The Municipality, which has its seat at Gardola, is formed by several villages.

HISTORY.
The first inhabitants of these rocky zones were probably the Galli-Genomani: one of their Gods was Bergino to whom small temples were erected. Under Tiberius, during the Roman invasion, the hamlet was aggregated to Brescia. In 1212 its economy improved considerably thanks to the Counts of Lodrone, masters of Bagolino, who had got their estate here. At the end of the XIV cent., different dominations caused the economic decadence of this hamlet by very heavy impositions. In 1385 Tignale passed under the Visconti and in 1404 it became again a feud of the Bishop of Trento and three years later it was inserted among the dominations of the "Serenissima" (Venice). The emperor Maximilian rode through these villages with his army in 1509. In 1700, by the treaty of Campoformio the stream Gardola traced out the boundaries between the Austro-Hungarian empire and the Cisalpine Republic.

TO SEE.
The Sanctuary of Madonna di Monte Castello, a national monument on the rock leaning out for 77 m on the lake. Inside there are frescoes of the school of Giotto and copper tables of Palma the Young.

Sanctuary of Monte Castello.
On this delightful hillock, by popular tradition, there was the altar to the pagan god Bergimo of the ancient Cenomani, the first inhabitants of Tignale, later changed into Mary's altar by the patient apostolate of the martyr St. Virgil (380-405 A.C.), the bishop of Trento. The people of Trento, on this rocky spur of primary strategic importance, in the year 1000, built a fortress which belonged to them until 1349, in front of the little temple.
It underwent many historical events during the centuries; it passed under the Scaligeri's rule, the duke of Milan Gian Galeazzo Visconti's in 1385, Pandolfo Malatesta's and again the Scaligeri's until 1797. The transformation of the castle into a temple began for the bishop of Brescia Berardo Maggi's wish after the battle between the people of Brescia and Trento on the 13th March 1283.

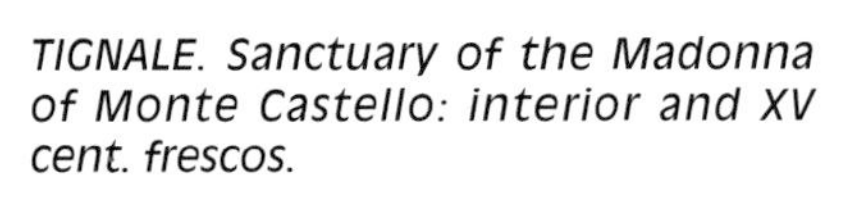

TIGNALE. Sanctuary of the Madonna of Monte Castello: interior and XV cent. frescos.

TIGNALE. Sanctuary of the Madonna of Monte Castello.

TREMOSINE

It is placed on a green tableland with rocky walls almost perpendicularly on the Lake; from this terrace stretching as far as Limone, you can admire wonderful panoramas. The town and its clusters of houses can be reached from the port of Campione through a road climbing up the flanks of the mountain to penetrate into the suggestive ravine of Brasa.

HISTORY.

It was undoubtedly the beauty of the place to draw an Etruscan population in a very ancient epoch. Its presence is revealed by the famous memorial tablet of Voltino (kept in the museum of Brescia) a real puzzle for palaeographers and philologists: the first four lines are in Latin, the last two in Etruscan or in the dialect of a primitive people. There are traces of other periods and of very industrious peoples: the castle (only some remains) and the church of Pieve (VI cent.) keeping intaglio works. The economy of the country was very prosperous, thanks to a manganese mine now disappeared. They mention the artisans' shops for the construction of mirrors.

TREMOSINE. Vertiginous viewpoint overhanging the lake.

TO SEE.
The Parish Church of Pieve.

The Parish Church of Tremosine is one of the most ancient of the west Gardesana road; it rises on a rocky spur leaning out on the lake. The church built about the end of the IV century AC was renewed many times; the bell tower, a square-shaped tower with a conical dome, was added to the temple in the X century AC.
In 1712 the dean Don Rambottini carried out the enlargement of the church with a new span and the sacristy. Inside there are the interesting intaglios of the organ of the VII century; the choir seats and the table in the sacristy, very fine intaglio, works of baroque style by Giacomo Lucchini from Condino, an more recent.

TREMOSINE. Parish Church: the chest in the sacristy by G. Lucchini.

TREMOSINE. Parish Church: High Altar.

LIMONE

It is a characteristic, picturesque village leaning out on the lake in a suggestive inlet among gardens, olive and lemon plantations. It enjoys a very mild climate. Its small, rustic houses, the small, pretty harbour, the narrow roads, give a characteristic note to this place much frequented by tourists. Limone has recently had a great increase in tourist and hotel equipment and now it is one among the most comfortable places of the lake.

HISTORY.
Its name derives perhaps from limen, frontier, or from the cultivation of lemons that once were tilled here. Already in 1000 we have news of this country; in 1200 Brescia had to defend it from the feudatories of Arco. The small town still keeps that particular charm described by D.H. Lawrence that conquered Ibsen, too. Daniele Comboni, missionary in Africa and the founder of the Colombian Order, was born in a villa among the olive trees in Tesol locality.

LIMONE. The port.

LIMONE. A delightful view through the luxuriant vegetation.

LIMONE. The lakeside.

TO SEE.
The parish church of the XVII cent. with the beautiful pictures of Celesti and an artistic wood crucifix of the XVII cent.; S. Rocco Church (XIV cent.); S. Pietro del Moro Church (XIII cent.); S. Giovanni Bridge; Bettoni Palace; Finance Palace.

St. Benedict's church was built in 1685 in place of a more ancient one (IX-X cent.). From 1693 to 1709 five altars were built inside, four with valuable-making marble, one with scagliola, with arabesques of great value.
Noteworthy are: Andrea Celesti's pictures (XVIII century), the high altar-piece ascribed to Veronese's school, the statue of the Virgin of Graces (XV cent.), a boxwood crucifix of the XVIII century. In the sacristy, a table, a valuable intaglio work of baroque style by Giacomo Lucchini from Condino (1718) with finely worked drawers and wickets.

LIMONE. Reflections on the lake.

LIMONE. Picturesque houses.

LIMONE. The Church of S. Rocco (XIV cent.). High Altar.

HOTEL LE PALME
RISTORANTE

RIVA DEL GARDA

It is an important, frequented tourist centre the north part of the lake stretching from the slopes of mount Rocchetta to mount Brione that divides it from Torbole. It enjoys a mild climate that favours a luxuriant vegetation. The promenade along the lake is among the most beautiful and elegant. Many roads depart from Riva, that is an important cross roads; the most important are: the one for Trento, going through the beautiful valley of the river Sarca, and the one of Tonale that, in the first part, climbs among the rocks, perpendicularly to the lake, and reaches the lake of Ledro, where you can see the remains of a village of the stone age. At about 3.5 km from Riva there is the interesting "Varone falls" throwing down into a rocky gorge an interesting sight.

HISTORY.
Riva was certainly inhabited by the Romans as the numerous important archaelogical discoveries prove. The enigmatic memorial table by which Claudia Severa had charged the nautical boarding-school of Riva to fill her husband's tomb with flowers every year, is well known to the scholars. The town, if the memorial tablet is exact, was the seat of a Boarding School of Helmsen. We know, for certain, that the zone was ascribed to the Fabia tribe. The first official document remembering a Riva dates back to 983 when the emperor Ottone II commits the town to the care of the bishops of Verona. In the XII cent. the zone belonged to the Princeps, Bishops of Trento, later to the Scaligeri, the Visconti of Milan, the Counts

RIVA DEL GARDA. View of the old Bastion.

HOTEL
HOTEL SOLE

of Tirolo and in the XV cent. during the Venetian wars, it was theatre of sharp contentions. In 1441 by the peace of Cremona, it was given to the Venetians who rebuilt the Fortress, built the present City Hall, and the Bastion. The government of the Serenissima lasted till 1509, when the town was occupied by the troops of P.V. Giorgio III of Naydek. In 1521 it was again under the Church of Trento with Bernardo Clesio. In 1703 it suffered the ravaging of the French of general Vendome during the Spanish succession war. In 1796 it was occupied by Napoleon's troops, in 1806 it was aggregated to Baviera, and in 1810 to the Italic Reign; later it was reoccupied by Austria. After the war of 1915/18 it was annexed to the Reign of Italy.

TO SEE.
The suggestive Piazza Tre Novembre, near the lake, with porches of the XIV cent. was built by Guglielmo de Frissoni from Como. Then there are the City Hall, called once "Dei Provveditori" and the Pretorio Palace, built by the Scaligeri in 1383. Through the ancient Porta Bruciata, which opens between the two fine buildings, you can reach S. Rocco square still keeping the rustic-lordly aspect of the ancient Riva.
In "Tre Novembre" Square, eastward, there is the Apponale Tower (the symbol of Riva), 34 m high, built in the XII cent. and heightened in 1555.
Beyond the channel surrounding it there is a fortress of the XII cent. with four square angular towers, reduced to the height of the roofs in the Austrian remaking in 1850, except the corbelled Keep, which defends the drawbridge. It was enlarged by the Scaligeri, Visconti, Venetians, by Bernardo Clesio and transformed into barracks by the Austrians in the XIX cent. From the courtyard full of Roman remains you can go up to the municipal museum (the history of Riva is illustrated on the walls), the fortress gives hospitality to the

Auditorium, seat of concerts, several exhibitions and congresses.
Beyond the fortress, in a wonderful position, there are the east gate gardens and the olive beach. The baroque Inviolata Church, the most precious monument of Riva rises northward. It was built in 1611 thanks to Gaudenzio Madruzzo, governor of Riva and Arco.
Then there are the baroque church of the Assunzione della Beata Vergine Maria, S. Giuseppe and S. Michele churches.

The Church of the Inviolata. This is perhaps Riva's most precious monument. It was built in 1611, thanks to the impetus of Gaudenzio Mandruzzo, the governor of Riva and Arco. The church has an extremely elegant baroque style, owed, it is assured, to the design of a Portugese architect whose name has been lost. The influence of Spanish architecture stands out even in the external structure. On the inside, which is rich and sumptous, the stucco-work of Rieto is very vivid. The crucifix with the Madonna on the first altar on the left is worth noting; on the other three altars, the altar piece Palma il Giovane (S. Carlo Gerolamo, S. Onofrio). Among the painters who have frescoed this church are remembered: Turri d'Arezzo, Bartolomeo Mangiarino da Salò (a presbyterian), Pietro Ricchi called the Lucchese. Kept in the sacresty are wardrobes and furniture of a very fine carving, probably the work of carvers from Trento and the Val Gardena.

RIVA DEL GARDA. The dock, the lakeside and characteristic view.

TORBOLE

Two characteristic hamlets, the first at the mouth of the Sarca, the second on the north slopes of mount Baldo, form Torbole, a pretty village on the slopes of the rocky hill of Castel Penede, in a charming position and enjoys a mild climate with a luxuriant vegetation of palms, oleanders, olives, laurels. Goethe lived at Torbole and described the beauty of these places conquered by the wonderful sight of its nature. The small town, an important and frequented place has got excellent tourist and hotel equipment. The cluster of houses of Nago is remembered for the passage of the Venetian ships that from Mori were lifted up mount Baldo and let down into the lake before Torbole during a war between the Venetians and the Visconti which broke out in 1437.

HISTORY.
The name of Torbole is bound to the famous battle of 1439 that decided the passage of the whole zone from the Visconti to Venice. The undertaking was conceived by Francesco Sforza and led by Stefano Contarini. To transfer from the Adige to Garda, by land, six galleys and 25 boats, they employed two thousand oxen and one hundred people.

TO SEE.

The parish church of Torbole, consacrated to S. Andrea, on a height showing beautiful panoramas. The high altar-piece, representing S. Andrea's martyrdom, a masterpiece of the painter Cignaroli (1706-1770) from Verona is very valuable. The parish church of Nago with a fine portal of the Renaissance; a memorial tablet remembers the famous jurist Scipio Sighele. S. Zeno's Longobard church (Nago) on a hill near the Scaligeri tower. The small port of Torbole with the "House of Customs' duty"; the remains of Castel Penede; the "Giants' Boilers".

TORBOLE. Panoramic views.

MALCESINE

It is a picturesque small town, on the riviera of the east Gardesana, on the slopes of mount Baldo, among a luxuriant vegetation of olives, cypresses, oleanders. The castle of the Scaligeri of the XIII cent. rises on a promontory perpendicular to the lake.
Malcesine is a health-resort and a famous frequented tourist place. Mount Baldo cableway carries, in a short time, from the mediterranean climate of the lake to 1800 m in height showing beautiful panoramas. At the end of the promenade there is the wonderful bay with the small " Isle of Dream " one of the most charming places of the lake.

HISTORY.
Its etymology is not simple; perhaps Malcesine derives from Melissineum (bosom of the honey), or Malcesine (a strongly placed spot). Once it was a fortified place, defended by the fortress. Its population enjoyed great autonomy during several periods: the bishop of Verona, after 1000, granted it numerous rights so Pope Eugene III let its inhabitants use coins and measures of their own. But the history of Malcesine is particularly bound to the domination of the Scaligeri. It was in the XII cent. that, on a spur perpendicular to the waters, in a panoramic position, they built the Castle which was later partly destroyed and then rebuilt as you can see from the different styles of some parts. The domination of the Scaligeri was followed by Austria's for 16 years, by the

MALCESINE. The port.

MALCESINE. The Scaligero Castle (XIII-XIV cent.).

Visconti's and then the Carrara's. The republic of Venice let the population, confederated with other communes, form the "Gardesana of waters". It was a long, enlightened domination which left deep traces in the village. It lasted 450 years from 1351 to 1797 with the short interruptions of the Visconti, Maximilian d'Austria and the French from 1805 to 1814. After the fall of Venice it was under Austria until 1866, which transformed it into a fortress. It gave hospitality to many famous personages such as Goethe who started his voyage through Italy from the lake of Garda. On 13th September 1786, the poet visited Malcesine and the Castle and, struck by its beauty, drew a sketch on a sheet. The poet called the attention of people who thought him a spy and he was hardly able to prove his identity. The poet's passage is now remembered by a bust and several memorial tablets, among which the one walled in the inn of the town, near the town hall, where he lived.

TO SEE.
The Castle of the XIII cent., changed many times, is divided into the low small palace and the upper one and is formed by three yards; in the second there is a bust of Goethe. The most ancient part is formed by a stone square-embattled fence; the central one shows swallow-tailed battlments.
From the outer yard you can reach the small balcony with a beautiful sight on the bay. In the Castle there is a little museum keeping naturalistic collections and historical antiques. The Captains' Palace, near the port, seat of the Commune in 1500, was the residence of the Captain of the lake during the period of the Scaligeri, and of the Venetian Republic. The parish church with a famous " Deposition" by Gerolamo Libri.

Madonna del Rosario's Church with many marble works. The picturesque port of Cassone, a clus-

ter of houses of Malcesine. Beyond Cassone there is the islet of Trimellone where in the X cent. rose a castle destroyed in 1158 by Barbarossa. Now the islet, once an Italian fort, shows a desolate aspect owing to the burst of explosions during the last war.

Parish Church. The XVI century parish church stands up among the low topped olive trees. It is particularly richly endowed with works of art and with many precious marbles (note the marble throne of the high altar of 1796, used to display the Holy Sacrament). In front of the shrine the statue with Christ in the tomb between angels and the arch of the patron saints of the Church, Benigno and Caro. The two saints are also portrayed on the altar-piece by Brusasorci. The frescoes representing the Deposition (the work of Girolamo dei Libri) were brought here from the Church of Santa Maria of the Organ in Verona. Noteworthy works by the painters Felice Boscaratti (Elisha and Rebecca, Abigail and David), Cialfini (altar-piece of Saints Benigno and Caro), and Odoardo Perini (in the Presbytery).

Church of the Madonna of the Rosary. Built in 1600, and also known as Madonna of the Fountain, from the fountain in the square opposite. This Church also has a number of outstanding works in marble (the eighteenth century High Altar). Some interesting paintings of the 1600's and 1700's (Madonna and Child and Saints Nicolò da Tolentino and S. Rocco; the work of Nicolò Crontani).

MALCESINE. Panorama.

TORRI DEL BENACO

It is one of the most characteristic villages of the Olive Riviera, placed at the foot of mount Baldo, in a wonderful zone among pines, olive and citron-groves. It is joined to Maderno, on the west bank of the lake, by a ferry-boat service for people and cars.

HISTORY.
The Romans called it "Castrium Turrium" for its numerous towers. It had great importance in the Middle Ages, in fact it was the chief town of the "Gardesana of the Lake" and the seat of the General Council, before this Council passed to Garda. "The Captain of the Lake" gathered the General Council, formed by the 18 confederated countries, to decide the management of the incomes, the defence of rights, the abolition of abuses. You can see some remains of the Roman "castra" in the square of the church where Berengario dated six royal diplomas from Torri in 1009. In 1383 Antonio della Scala rebuilt the manor-house of which we have three towers, among which a Roman one, with other interesting remains.
The philosopher and mathematican Domizio Calderini, died in Rome in 1487, was born here.
He is remembered in a marble stele near the Trinity's small church, with an inscription by Poliziano. Among the famous men who lived in Torri, we remember Andrè Gide who spent, as he wrote in his diary, "wonderful days here from June to September, in 1948".

TO SEE. The Trinity's small church, in Calderini square, with frescoes of the school of Giotto; the facade of the XVIII cent., of Eccheli Palace with "the small house of the XV cent."; Berengario's Tower, in Church Square, well preserved remains of the Roman "Castrum Turrium" and the Roman quarter ("el trincerone"); the Duomo, known for the variety of the marbles used in the altars.

TORRI DEL BENACO. Panorama and the Scaligero Castle.

PUNTA SAN VIGILIO

In the bright blue of the lake there is the promontory of Punta S. Vigilio shaping two delightful inlets: one, known with the name of "Bay of the Sirens" with a small beach, the other shapes a small pretty harbour. On the cape of the promontory, among olive-groves and cypresses, there is the ancient small church of St. Vigilio and the nice Villa Guarienti erected in the 16th century designed by Sanmicheli, with a wonderflul park adorned with statues.

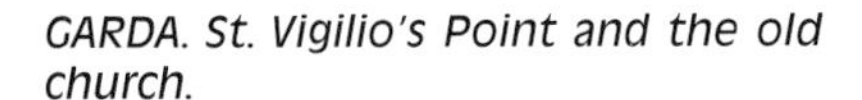

GARDA. St. Vigilio's Point and the old church.

GARDA

It lies in the middle of a wonderful gulf with very curved banks and is protected, northward by the slopes of mount Baldo, southward by the fortress, and eastward by slow, moraine heights.
The Gardesana route, among villas and olive yards unites the town to S. Vigilio headland, one of the most famous places of the lake, much frequented by Italian and foreign tourists. A carriageable asphalted road goes from Garda to "Spiazzi di Monte Baldo" and the famous Madonna della Corona Sanctuarv.

HISTORY.
Some traces of the neolithic period installations were found on the fortress. In witness of the ancient inhabitants of these zones there are also rock inscriptions found in S. Vigilio. Pagus Romano got a great importance in the Middle Ages because of its castle when Charlemagne changed it into a country in 768. From that time Garda gave the name to the Lake, once called Benaco. According to a legend the nuptials of the first of the barbarian queens of Carducci, Teodolinda, were celebrated here. In 950 Queen Adelaide from Borgogna, Lotario's widow, was kept prisoner in the Fortress by Berengario II; she succeded in escaping thanks to the help of a fisherman or a friar and took refuge at Canossa, marrying Ottone I from Germania, who exiled Berengario, on Christmas evening in 951. Turisendo, a feudal vassal of Gardesana held out to Barbarossa's

GARDA. Panoramic views and Villa Albertini.

siege (1162-63) from the fortress. This memorable resistance is remembered also by Muratori: "No town in Italy resisted to this terrible Augustus, except the Fortress of Garda". The vicissitudes of the Fortress are bound to Ottone of Wittesbach, the founder of the House of Baviera and to the Bishop Alberto di Trento, till 1209 when Ottone IV, after taking it to the Commune, destroyed it. Also the rule of the Venetian Republic left important traces. In 1452 the "Antichi Originari" Corporation bought the fishing rights for 3075 gold ducats; to pay that amount the women had to sell their jewels. The history and legends of Garda were summed up by the poet Carducci in famous lines.

TO SEE.
The ancient hamlet with its characteristic lanes; the two well-preserved gates of the medieval fencing wall (inside the west gate there is an elegant mullioned window with two lights), The Gothic-Venetian palace of the Captain of the Serenissima on the small square looking over the lake.
Palace Fregoso where Bandello found hospitality; perhaps the novel of Juliet and Romeo was born here. Along the lake there is San Micheli's loggia of the XVI cent. with a low tower.
On the Gardesana road there is the interesting Villa Albertini, shaped like a castle, surrounded by a large park where on 10th June 1848 King Carlo Alberto received the delegation bringing him the annexation act of Lombardy to Piedmont. Other interesting buildings are: Palazzo Carlotti (1500), Palazzetto del Ponte (1700) Villa Canossa, Villa Guarienti (to S. Vigilio). The parish church keeps some paintings of Palma il Giovane and Francesco Paglia.

Viila Guarienti, built in 1500 by Sanmicheli for the Veronese writer Agostino Brenzone (not open to visitors). Making a part of the villa is the small, ancient Church of S. Vigilio surrounded by cypresses, which, with its little bell tower reflected in the lake, is an inexhaustible source of inspiration for painters. At the tiny, characteristic port with an inn nearby, it is possible to hire a boat from which to admire the famous view of the little church, from the lake.
Beyond the Punta (Point) occupied by the magnificent park of Villa Guarienti, the idyllic Bay of the Sirens, with its limpid waters between olive and cypress trees, is particularly inviting for a bath.
The painter Pisanello (1379-1455) was born in S. Vigilio.

GARDA. Picturesque view.

PIAZZA CATULLO
AV 5038

BARDOLINO

It lies in a wonderful position at the foot of hills covered with orchards, olive yards and vineyards producing famous wines. Its position, its very mild climate, the wide beaches and its environs draw tourists and holiday-makers.

HISTORY.
According to some glottologists, its name derives from the German, Bardali or Pardali, king Argonauta Auleto's daughter. But before getting a name, Bardolino was inhabited by populations who already knew the famous wine celebrated during the Roman period, the prehistoric remains found here, prove it. It was famous for its wine, which was celebrated by Cato and Cassiodoro and won the tables of Caesar and Catullus who lived between Verona and Sirmione and knew the zone well. The streets of Bardolino still show the Roman mark as well its toponymy which keeps latin words, certain distances, between two houses, are still called "intercapedines". The name of Bardolino appears for the first time in 807 in a document signed by King Pipino, Charlemagne's son, in his residence in Verona. During the Middle Ages it was a free Commune, then it passed under the Scaligeri and Venice. The passage of the Lansquenets (1526) who spread grief and ruin is remembered by documents. Under the rule of Venice, Bardolino got a happy development of agriculture and viticulture. Among its famous personages there are the three Betteloni poets, Cesare (1808-58), Vittorio (1840-1910) and Gianfranco (1876-1948), father, son and

BARDOLINO. The center, the Church of San Severo (XI-XII cent.) and the port.

CURA DELL'UVA
GRAPE CURE
BARDOLINO
RISTORANTE
AREA
PEDONALE

nephew. We know the famous, short poem "The Lake of Garda" by Cesare Betteloni, a commendation of the great lake and its people.

TO SEE.
S. Severo Roman church with a Longobard crypt (VIII cent.) and frescoes of the XII cent., S. Zeno Longobard church of the VIII cent.

Church of San Severo (XI-XII cent.). An old Romanesque construction of the XI century, it was part of the very ancient Pieve di Garda mentioned in the Diploma of Berengaria in 983 AD. Restored in the XII century, in the XV it became a parish church. Then it neglected and lost its importance during the following centuries. The church has three unequal apses and a number of embrasure windows at the sides. In the interior interesting frescoes represent the visions of the Apocalypse and figures of Apostles and Saints paintings going back to the XIII century.

CISANO DI BARDOLINO

Church of Santa Maria (XI-XII cent.). The first church was built around 915 on the ruins of a pagan temple, it was rebuilt in the XII century after the earthquake of 1117. An interesting Romanesque style prothyrum or hanging porch projects above the door in the façade. A fresco of a Madonna and Child painted in the niche is from about 1500. Some VIII century sculptures decorate the sides of the prothyrum: an eagle, a fish, a horse, and a horseman. Above a two-light window decorated with friezes and dentils and three finely worked stones.
The really important apse is a true jewel of Romanesque art.

BARDOLINO. Promenade along the lake.

BARDOLINO. The port.

LAZISE

It is a picturesque hamlet surrounded by the ancient walls with embattled towers, built by the Scaligeri. Lazise which keeps so many memories of its medieval past, is now the goal of numerous tourists drawn by its wonderful position; in fact it is one among the most beautiful and interesting places of the lake.

HISTORY.
Lazise, Lasitium for the Romans had a very eventful history. The "Corporation of the Natives", the prevailing class of the village, built S. Nicolò's small church in a fine, Roman style in 1100. In the XI cent., they built the castle, one of the most interesting of the lake Garda, where the sovereigns of the Holy Roman Empire lived. It was enlarged by the Scaligeri and the Venetians. Later it was destroyed and in XIX cent. it was very important under the rule of the Serenissima, for Venice had got an important shipyard here, interred with the ancient port.

TO SEE.
S. Nicolò's Roman church with a very characteristic façade, regular below and formed by broken pieces of earthenware above.
Inside it keeps frescoes looking like Pisanello's style. The ancient Custom-house near the Port, built by Venetian trusses; the Roman tower in the churchyard; if you want, you can visit the Scaligeri's Castle by the keepers' leave.
The Castle, the Towers and the embattled walls which surrounded the old Village. The external walls

LAZISE. The old customs station and the Church of St. Nicholas.

LAZISE. The lakeside.

were protected by a deep moat. There were three entrance gates to the Castle: one on the east, the San Zeno Gate (with a mosaic of the Saint); one on the north, the Cansignorio Gate (1375-1376); one on the south, the Gate of the Lion of St. Mark (1405-1797). The first gate was used by the inhabitants and goods waggons, the other two by the garrison.

The sanctuary of the Madonna of Frassino.
A few kilometres from Peschiera, in a lovely inland position, beside the motorway "Serenissima", stands the sanctuary of the Madonna of Frassino. Here on the 11th May 1510, in extremely sad times of war between Venetians, Spanish, French and Germans, the wonderful event witnessed by a pesant, Bartolomeo Broglia, took place. Broglia was working in a vineyard in the Pigna quarter, when, writes the historian Antonio Fappani, he was terrified by the sight of a big snake. He immediately thought of a prayer to the Madonna and suddenly there appeared right in front of his eyes, among the leaves of an ash tree, a statue of the Virgin, surrounded by light. Ecstatically he fell to his knees giving thanks, and after having kissed the statue he took it home, shutting it in a box. When he went to take it out he found it was gone. The statue had miraculously returned to the ash tree of the marvel. The good Broglia, holding himself unworthy, recounted the story to the archpriest of Peschiera, don Antonio Cornacchi, who went with the authorities to the place of the apparition. With a solemn procession the statue was transported to Peschiera to the church of the Discipline. But even from there it dissapeared to return to the ash tree of the miracle. It was decided to build a sanctuary on the spot. Work began on the 10th September 1511 and as soon as the temple was finished it was trusted to the Serviti, passing, a few years later, to the Minori monks. The monument restored in 1931 to its primitive franciscan beauty, holds numerous works of art: a table by Zeno da Verona (1541), a nativity by Paolo Farinati (1560), other works by Farinati and by Astolfi. The 18th century medallions among the archs of the side chapel and the painting above the central door are by Giovanni Simbenati. The heart of the sanctuary is represented by the chapel where the miraculous statue is kept. The altar-piece is still Farinati's (1560), while the twelve paintings of the face and the walls are eleven by Bertanza da Salo (XVIII century) and the twelth, depicting the blessed Duns Scoto, is by Zambrognini. The two bronze statues are by prof. R. Banterle.

LAZISE. Scaligero Castle.

LAZISE. The wet dock and the Church of St. Nicholas.

PESCHIERA

It is an important tourist and commercial centre on the south-east end of the lake where the river Mincio flows down. The fortress with the ramparts, the high walls and deep ditches surrounding it give the fine, small town an imposing, austere look.

HISTORY.
The events of Peschiera, as the remains discovered during the excavations of the XIX cent. prove, vanish in prehistory. It still existed with the name of "Africa" in the Roman period, and was the seat of a seamans' school. Some historical testimonies remember the stay of Caius Marius, who settled in the fortress when he had to fight against Cimbri (101 BC).
It was always a contended centre owing to the strategic importance of its port; in 849 the navy of Peschiera was destroyed by the inhabitants of Verona and the Venetians. It belonged to the Scaligeri (1409), the Gonzaga (1441), Venice (1584-1659). In 1530 Charles V, returning from his coronation in Bologna, stayed in Peschiera from 20th to 21st April, receiving the Venetians' homage. The town was enlarged and fortified under the Serenissima, according to the plans of Guidobaldo della Rovere and Sanmicheli. In June 1796 Napoleon fixed his headquarters here. After Campoformio, the fortress passed under Austria.
Alexander I from Russia, the Grand Duke of Tuscany, the King of Naples lived here, during the Congress of Vienna. It was fortified afrer the armistice of Villafranca and remained under Austria until 1866 and became one of the

PESCHIERA. Betteloni Cesare square.

PESCHIERA. The port.

Garda Sport

fourth fortified towns of the famous Quadrilateral with Verona, Mantua and Legnano. In the fortress of Peschiera, King Victor Emmanuel III decided to resist, to the last, on the line of Piave on 8th November 1917.

TO SEE.
The double fencing wall (2250 metres long) and the remains of the fortress. The historical small palace, a work of Sanmicheli, with the famous Congress Hall, keeps antiques of the Renaissance and the war of 1915-18. On the façade there is a memorial tablet of P. Canova, remembering the meeting of the allies on 8th November 1917.

PESCHIERA. Betteloni Cesare square.

PESCHIERA. The sanctuary of the Madonna del Frassino (XVI cent.).

PESCHIERA. Characteristic spot.

PIZZERIA
STOP

© EDITIONS KINA ITALIA / EuroGrafica - Italy
Printing by KINA ITALIA / EuroGrafica - Italy
Exclusive sales agent - Poiatti Pietro - Nave (BS)
Text by Francesco Martello
All rights reserved for texts and photograph.
Full or partial reproduction is prohibited.